Unearthing the Black Woman

Reflections, Affirmations, and Poetry

Vol. I

UNEARTHING THE BLACK WOMAN
Reflections, Affirmations, & Poetry, Vol I.

ISBN:978-0-578-39927-0

Come & Sit with Me

Close your eyes for a moment and breathe

Relax with me

This is your time, the moment to recalibrate your mind,
your heart, and your spirit

Releasing all judgment of self and others

Receiving that which is yours

Aligned within

Inside and out

Reflecting on the lessons learned from your past

As you walk in awareness, self-love, and

self-kindness in this present moment

Now prepare for the birthing and blooming of your future

Love & Blessings,

MK

CONTENTS

ACKNOWLEDGMENTS

To my children who saw my strength even when I was weak.

To my dear friend Dawn who encouraged me to live my life.

To my one and only champion Michael who continually shows me what unconditional love looks like,

To those who always believed in me & saw my inner light as a guiding star.

To my mom who taught me to never give up...

UNEARTHING THE BLACK WOMAN
Reflections, Affirmations, & Poetry, Vol I.

INTRODUCTION

In the depths of life's journey, we often discover the treasures hidden within. Like a skilled archaeologist unearthing long-forgotten relics, we dig deep, assisted by the flickering light of our resilience.

After my divorce, homelessness, depression, and the sting of abandonment, I found myself at a crossroads. It was a pivotal moment that forced me to confront the impact of my choices that led to my pain and circumstances. The mirror reflected a stark truth: I had been wearing a mask, clinging to an illusion of a fairytale that had robbed me of my identity and stifled my existence.

This awakening became the catalyst for change, igniting a profound expedition of self-reflection and healing through writing. I picked up the pen again, reclaiming my voice and unburdening my spirit. The words flowed, carrying the weight of my experiences and the wisdom gained through hardship. Through this process, I grieved for my lost life and the illusions that had kept me complacent.

Through my writing, I invite others to embark on their personal excavation to uncover the obscured gems within. I explore interrelated themes: of resilience, healing, and the power of embracing one's true self. Together, we can survey the layers, navigate the hills and valleys, and rediscover the rare and overlooked splendor within each of us. Together let us embrace the power of truth, vulnerability, and authenticity.

I emerged from the ashes of my former self, having experienced spiritual, emotional, mental, and financial death. It was a necessary demise, a life-changing process I hesitated to share and felt shame in uttering until now. This book became my companion in my passage of rebirth, my spiritual doula, guiding me through the unearthing of something greater than myself.

Its rhythm extends beyond my narrative, touching the lives of black women, all women, and men, universally encompassing our past, present, and future.

Countless nights I sat, burdened, and plagued by hopelessness, aimlessness, and loneliness. I longed for the discomfort to end, yearning for something new, something different. In those moments, I realized that only I could walk in my shoes and fulfill my unique destiny and purpose.

I wholeheartedly believe that my life is part of a collective, a valuable lesson meant to empower others to embrace their scars and start on their healing journeys. This book serves as the opening chapter of my story, a lyrical fragment woven into the rich tapestry of ongoing discussions. Its goal is to help us accept ourselves, heal, and uncover the treasure within ourselves. There is a sacred space where we learn, support, share, and prosper.

Each day, we move through the layers of life and recognize its influence. We discern which layers have inflicted more harm than good. In a society that often marginalizes women and demands our adaptation. It is crucial that we extend compassion and grace to every aspect of who we are.

Let us find the courage to let go of what does not build us or bring healing to our lives. Finding peace within ourselves may be a challenge for some, while others may experience change with ease. However, together, we can move mountains. We can liberate and elevate not only our sisters but also our brothers, lovers, kinfolk, and even strangers.

Our voices hold tremendous power, but through our actions, we shape our identity, determine our direction, and manifest our potential.

May my words evoke reflection, offer guidance, foster self-love, and inspire you to embrace your unique essence as we navigate life with purpose and intention. Remember, you are never alone, whether in the highest of highs or lowest of lows.

As you read this book, the path you traverse within these pages is in your hands. Open your heart and mind, embrace what resonates, and release what doesn't serve you.

May you continue to grow, evolve, and bloom on this transformative quest called life.

With love and blessings,

~MK

CHAPTER 1
ROOTED

Fixed in one's position

Unearthed Vessel

She runs her calloused hands,
Along the weathered handle,
And with purpose, she glides them.
Along the cold, unwavering metal frame.

The weight of the sturdy shovel anchors her,
Compels her to remember the urgency,
To unearth the torment of affliction.
She laughs softly, masking her disdain.

With each deep breath,
She plunges the shovel into the waiting earth.
Digging relentlessly into a place,
She refuses to ignore.

For healing beckons from afar,
Love yearns to enfold her,
Offering a path to escape.
Bitterness, hauntings, and tragedies are unveiled.

On this journey, she is her hero,
She knows it well, with every fiber of her being,
Each bend in her back signifies strength.
Her arms carry resilience and might.

Removing every obstacle,
That dares to threaten her peace.
Alone, she persists, delving deeper.
Smashing through walls of falsity.

Amongst the solitude and disunity,
She rediscovers the essence of her spirit,
Once again, intuition guides.
Jaded thoughts are released.

Words of deprivation, she chooses to discard.
The hole grows deeper with each thrust.
Sweat on her brows, and dirt adorns her face.
On her knees, she finds humility and faith.

Grace and mercy support her from within,
Tapping into her inner divinity,
She reaches deep, unearthing her true self.
Her spirit awakened a profound transformation.

Madness of Life

But for a moment, I submit to the madness of life,
Embracing the mysterious forces,
That dwell in the unknown.

Releasing what I once believed was destined,
Bearing my vulnerabilities and exposing my soul.
My words take on new forms,
A metamorphosis.

Blossoming like a rose, once beneath the fertile ground,
Nature grants permission for my energy to rise.
A sacred transmission, a tender invitation,
Have you gazed into my eyes?

I close them, projecting myself into higher realms,
Beyond shapes, beyond time, and faces.
Engaging with boundless energy, fueled by courage,
Hope becomes my refrain, and my map a melody.

Our lives unfold as stories,
Painting the world's canvases,
Do we dwell in illusions, a multiverse, or confusion?

Is existing, a fusion of flesh and spirit,
Love and hate?
Mercy and grace entwined,
While others negotiate?

Amidst the vibrations of faith, we raise our eyes,
Even when fear lurks in our hearts.
For the sake of Heaven, we remain grounded,
Welcoming the sound of a new day, a new path.

We push forward, expressing gratitude,
Thankful to the Creator for the gift of life.
"I am that I am," a profound truth resonates within,
Understanding now all that is, was, and ever will be.

Listen closely to the ancestral drums,
As they beat.
Transcending the boundaries of universal happiness,
In a realm beyond comprehension, we exist.

We are everlasting energy, which never ends.

Loneliness
Lyrical Reflection

What is loneliness? A reminder that we continue to look outwards and not inwards? We may have people around us and still lack a deeper connection. Finding ourselves yearning for what we find through the master of oneself. We have been born into this earth with the need to belong, to need physically and connect with each other. However, our main connection should start inwardly.

Wandering without expectation, shattered from the rocks of life, ceasing to climb to higher heights or survey the depths.

At times we may negate the work to uncover what's hidden underneath, it's not easy. We may blindly seek after that which we see with our eyes and ignore what we know within our higher selves.

Many people forget who they came here to be, unable to find purpose. Is it possible that our loneliness derives from not walking in our destined path? Unseen wealth within is waiting to be found. We know there is power in our words to speak life, to tear down or create. To manifest beyond human sight. Cascading waves of sound, we choose to swim and refuse to drown.

Bliss is fleeting, yet worth repeating it runs haphazardly unreprimanded.

Our minds would love to upper hand it, so we often analyze and sabotage, reading between the lines. Dopamine overload.

Stories progress, and truth be told, the phone call is still on hold. However, we can pick up the receiver. Choose to dismantle the weight of the past like slicing meat with a cleaver. No longer playing small, no leave it to beaver. We recognize the call, yeah, A self-believer. Going after what's ours like a golden retriever. No longer comparing, staring, and demeaning oneself. Being comfortable within and taking our dreams off the shelf. It's not automatic, we are the spark, we are the magic, with us is where it starts.

Become

She perceived it clearly,
The rigid confines of stereotype,
That replayed relentlessly in her mind,
No room for nuances,
No shades of gray or vibrant haze.

Forced to confront the truth,
That she was black,
Black like the smokestacks,
Emitting from the ashes of Black Wall Street.

Black like the soil,
Embedded in the enslaved feet,
Black like the skin,
Of bodies hung from poplar trees.

She was made to see,
All the negativity that society projected,
Yet unwilling to accept,
The self-imposed poverty of perception.

She tilted her head, once held high,
When she reached her mother's thighs,
And sighed...

"This cannot define my reality,"
For within her, the universe stirred,
Creating a resistance,

What she saw began to lose its power,
As she stood quietly, refusing to cower.

She started to witness the beauty,
In all creations of life,
Realizing she could heal and be free,
Spreading her wings wide.

Because she was...
Black like the night,
Enveloping the earth,
Majestic, residing within galaxies.

Black like the eagle,
Soaring with purpose and grace,
Foreseeing its plans,
Executing its strategies.

Black like obsidian,
Guarding, cleansing the old,
Nurturing personal and spiritual growth.

Black like the Stallion,
Unyielding, resilient, and determined,
Refusing to succumb to defeat.

She shed tears... not of regret,
But for the rewritten history by strangers,
Stripped from her forefathers,
Their struggles devalued and demeaned.

She wept, for she nearly lost her identity,
For which countless lives were sacrificed,
She wept, for she almost fell in love,
With the captive's lies, my, my, my.

Oh, wipe those tears and rise,
It's never too late to open your eyes,
Behold the truth of your conception,
Embrace the being you were meant to be,

Unleash your spirit and become...

Unapologetically

I'm sorry, I don't apologize,

For the way, my hips sway,
And my nose rests gently and wide upon my face.
My lips comprise their shape,
And my body curves like Frito lay.

I'm sorry, I don't apologize.

For me speaking my truth,
For learning from my youth,
That I can't remain around you and your toxicity,
Your negative, critical nature,
I wave away like vapors.

Cause I don't have time for nonsense,
I'm sorry, I don't apologize.

For the tears I've cried,
For being denied, rejected, and molested,
For the wounds caused by brothers,
Who should have protected?

For being treated like trash,
And taking the time to heal me,
With love, prayer, and meditation.
Not afraid to do therapy and take some medication,
Pursue what I love or take a vacation.

I'm sorry, I don't apologize.

UNEARTHING THE BLACK WOMAN
Reflections, Affirmations, & Poetry, Vol I.

For not fitting in your box,
Wearing crop tops and Bantu knots,
Creating lanes and dreaming dreams,
That is far beyond average.
You say I'm a savage.

Because I refuse to be who you want,
I intend to keep my head lifted high,
Sip my tea and watch Queen Sugar late at night.
Write my poetry, sing my songs,
How I like.

I'm sorry, I don't apologize.

For loving to see others win,
Taking a sip of gin and scratching a lotto ticket,
Now and then.
For loving hard,
For being stubborn yet willing to learn.

To pray for you and others,
Overcoming the sting of guilt and shame,
Never again limiting my views.
Taking space and advocating change,
No matter what the obstacle,

We will see it through.
I'm sorry, I don't apologize.

Choose love or Choose war?

It happened, I was transported from home base,
Awaiting my purpose, a mission unknown.
Isolated once more, my memories grew dim,
Longing for a place I could hardly remember within.

Haunted by familiarity, the blinding glimmer,
Like December's snow, coldness taking flight.
Where are the embers, the spiritual flame?
The abandoned womb, devoid of its claim.

Dependent on those who walked the path before,
Destined for greatness, a choice to adore or abhor?
Decisions and choices, piled at my door,
Destined for greatness, choose love, or choose war?

Power, greed, slander, and disgrace,
Ego and pride are the culprits we chase.
Religion, politics, history's bitter taste,
The ache of slavery was inflicted with haste.

But what of our future, what awaits in store?
Destined for greatness, love, or war to explore?
Stand tall, for the family has weathered the storm.
Rebuilding, shifting, fighting, a unity reborn.

Reclaiming what was taken,
With resilience in our core.
Yet in the face of greatness,
Love, or war we must adore.

The time will come, as the rocket ship soars,
To return us home, as nothing else endures.

And in the end, when were unable to run.
What will persist is the residue we've spun.
Did we choose love in the battles we bore?
Or did we succumb to the ravages of war?

Homage to our Ancestors and the Black Arts Movement
(1965-1975)

The creative ones,
They are the wind that rises beneath our feet,
The freedom that kisses our skin,
Refusing defeat, discrete.

We linger in their presence,
We can breathe at ease,
Understanding that we are still developing,
Knowing and progressing; consciousness.

Our chest expresses that life is within reach,
Artistic beings,
Fluid and never flinching,
Inch by inch, a collective transaction.

A movement of strength, liberation, and expansion,
We build without measures,
Boldly facing the debate.

They boogie right beside us,
Their words glide in stride,
Their wisdom resides connected,

Deep, deep inside us.

Humility and confidence, dismantling pride,
The sounds of everlasting minds,
Priceless, ageless, fragrant, and bliss
Echoes of mercy and melanin dipped.

Royal excellence, gifts of love,
My brothers and sisters, an extension from,
Exponential factors that share a hereafter,
A legacy, a masterpiece, exemplified.

Creating a sweet aroma.

My Mother, the Beginning

Where can I find the starting point,
When I contemplate,
The countless sacrifices,
You've made.

The unwavering love you've bestowed upon me,
Even in moments of disagreement and discord,
You offered prayers on my behalf,
When darkness veiled my path, obscuring the glow.

You fueled my hope as it waned in haste,
Speaking words of life, uplifting my spirit,
Through widowhood's sorrow,
You stood by my side.

In the depths of my divorce, devoid of judgment,
You offered support,
though you may not have understood,
Your unwavering presence, a steadfast rock.

My mother, an anchor in the violent sea,
My beloved mother,
I express my gratitude,
In times of fear, you stood resolute.

Tuned in to the whispers of the ancestors,
A visionary,
A selfless provider,
My Mother.

You taught life,
Through the melody of your existence,
Counseled by faith's unwavering compass,
And your prayers served as reminders,
To the heavens of your heartfelt desires.

I am thankful,
I am grateful,
For the privilege of calling you,
My mother.

Give Up?

What does it mean to give up?
The mere sound of this phrase,
Ushers in the faint memory of stubborn hiccups.

Evading my control,
Not giving them power or permission.
I have never been privy to such a notion,
That giving up was an option.

I settle upon the balcony of life,
Anchoring myself to its platform,
Above ground.

Higher than I want to be at times,
But I understand the effectiveness of foresight,
The willingness to expand,
And the strength to fight.

With all my might, with all my might.
Awareness heightened,
Within I had sunken to the lowest of lows.

Everywhere I looked,
Swift, heavy blows to my life force.
Left, right hooks, TKO.

Momentarily inundated,
My life ending that way,
It's never been slated.

So, I stand with a glove on each hand.
Lucidity does not deceive,
Even when shame, failure, or anger,
Come to mock me.

Past scars and agitation,
Want to rob my possessions,
Merely replaceable obsessions.

Succession-encoded,
Melanin loaded,
Engrafted into higher plains.

Transcontinental movements,
Planetary explosions,
I'm creating all this commotion.

Cause what does it mean to give up?
When for me as a black woman,
Giving up is not an option.

Identity
Reflection

Growing up in a religious environment, I only began to grasp the contrast between organized religion and spirituality as a young adult. It became clear to me that there was a profound distinction between religion as an institution and the intimate relation of a spiritual relationship. Often finding myself immersed in church settings, success seemed to hinge on people-pleasing through submission and servitude, satisfying the insatiable desire for acceptance.

However, as I turned the pages of my life, adulthood revealed that my inflicted wounds were from a place that was meant to provide healing and restoration. Inside the corridors judgment and disease thrived, with blame conveniently shifted onto external forces and little emphasis on self-responsibility. I found myself stuck in an unhealthy cycle, in need of change. What happens when we venture outside the confines of religion, searching for a deeper spiritual connection, only to have the layers of one's identity called into question?

As I uncovered the layers that influenced my life, I confronted an inquiry: Who was I outside of the congregation?

Who are we as individuals? If we don't find fulfillment in associations, or belonging within a religious institution, a relationship, career, or specific group of people?

In my sorrow, I discovered that the responsibility to seek our truth and solidify our identities belong to us. Everyone has the power to decide how they navigate life, reclaim their purpose, learn to love, and ultimately find inner peace.

We must search inward, understanding who we genuinely are. For we enter this world alone, and we will depart in the same manner. What or who shapes our values and personal beliefs?

Who's responsible?

In search of quietness, my mind offers no remorse,
A trojan horse, harboring digressions, of course.
Each echo grows louder, incessant sound,
I invested, lips sewn shut, no thread found.

I immerse my woes in the warmth of my head,
Ignoring the unseen, something within me spread.
Where is my blanket of false security, I plea?
Beneath its cover, I'll hide, safe from prying eyes.

With a fake smile and rolled-up sleeves, I prepare,
Armed with armor, ready to fend off thieves' snare.
I've given so much and received little in return,
Sacrificed, believing it was my duty to discern.

As a woman, I thought I must set myself aside,
For those I love, a duty I couldn't hide.
I birth ideas, pour into nations, and kneel for souls,
Shout for change, embracing humility's roles.

I love fiercely, at times recklessly, true,
Pulling loved ones from the fire, paying my dues.
Accountability and resilience, my luminosity,
Shouldering problems in the dark of night.

Weighted down for a season, but shall I rise?
Would it be treason to seek composure, to be wise?
In a moment, I reclaimed my self-composure.
Allowing love to flourish, a healthy exposure.

Agony and weakness require no atonement,
I am my opponent, with freedom of choice.
Moving beyond what I feel, what's best for me.
Facing tests, unyielding to whatever may be.

Highlighting internal components.
Zoning, flashes of truth,
Illuminate my brilliance.
Acknowledging weakness, finding resilience.

No need for blame, not here for show,
With free will, I transcend what I used to know.
Deciding what serves me, what brings me peace.
Passing every test, embracing life's lease.

CHAPTER 2
PRUNED

Cutting away that which is dead or overgrown to make room for increase or growth…

Trust Meter

My trust meter is broken.
And it hinders me from rising,
Extending my arms like branches,
Lifting my skirt high and dancing.

Prancing openly under the moon,
A lunatic romanced by Lo-fi Spotify.
Zoom meetings, I still modify.

My apprehension rises,
Humiliation comes to sit beside me.
Don't let Mr. Pride find me.
Cause inside me, greatness sits.

Energy in a pot with a sealed-up lid.
Wondering when all this sh*t will end.
Is coronavirus at it again?
Conspiracy reducing family and friends.

Let go of the frazzled ends.
Relationships that try to drown you,
Look down on you,
Shake you up and cause you to forget.

Quit all the antics.
Do something different, no need to panic.
Life is full of hills and gullies,
Rain, sun, Ak's, and Num-chunks.

My trust meter is broken.
There is nowhere to put a token.
Value comes from healing,
And those who take are only stealing.

From the surface of the matter,
The pain of my heartache goes splatter,
I set up these words to formulate an injunction.

Self-awareness needs no seduction.
There's no parking along this street,
Cause I am under construction.

Safe Mode
Reflection

Have you ever been wounded? Betrayed, lied on, cheated on, or talked about negatively?

Did those experiences cause you to become jaded, mistrustful, build walls, hold resentment, hate, or unforgiveness? Some of us have worked through them and maybe even let those situations and people go by releasing them. But what does the residue of these experiences look like? Are we free to trust again, love again, believe again? Do we hold these encounters unconsciously? Are we allowing them to foreshadow our future endeavors and relationships?

I remember a friend I had in my twenties that shared her doubts about her new boyfriend because of a past relationship. She shared that she played it safe to avoid being hurt but realized it enhanced her insecurities. She also created unnecessary conflict and fed into negative thoughts that had no merit.

Clearly, she was not giving this relationship a chance to develop because in safe mode, we are limited in how we function. We operate at a lower power, with minimal access to the things that we need.

Often, emitting at a lower negative frequency even though it is meant for our protection. Being stuck in safe mode can become crippling and keep one from reaching their pinnacle if no resolution is found.

Safe mode can be a place of safety if it's used correctly. I remember using the technical setting to troubleshoot and fix issues with the computer and then return it to its full state of operation. In that state we can fully exemplify who we are in our lives and relationships. A simple reminder that the real work must first be done inwardly. In safe mode, we can protect ourselves, troubleshoot, and fix the issues that caused us to enter that space. So, when we obtain healing, we will emerge into our rightful position. Presenting at full capacity and having everything we need.

Accountability

She's escaping this place within her mental.
Pent up frustrations, glazed eyes dilated.
Monsters of past ages.
Cocoa Butter and skin grazes.
Was it love? now, manipulation.
It's anger.
She feels it and grips it for a second.
Inhaling its fierceness,
And exhaling its pointless notions.
Concoctions mixed; an elixir fixed.
It is what it is.
He caused agony: she suppressed it.
She allowed it because she invested.
The only case is to digest it.
Excrete it out and remove its presence.
Accountability.

Accountability
Affirmations

I am a willing participant in my life.

I take ownership of my emotions and reactions,

knowing that I have control over how I respond.

I honor my commitments and follow through on my

promises.

I courageously dig beneath the soil of my heart,

mind, & spirit,

To identify the roots that I have allowed to provide

influence and direction to my existence.

I learn from my mistakes and use them as

opportunities for growth.

I understand that accountability is a key component

of personal empowerment and success.

I take accountability for myself.

Goodbye

I converse with you each passing day.
I engage with you, perhaps too much to say.
Now I realize your conniving plays.
Into my life, attempting to keep me astray.

You desire to keep me stagnant, in a loop.
Driving me towards madness, making me stoop.
Encouraging complaints, a never-ending soup.
Fear, it's time for you to pack up and scoot.

I've told you, my love, for you no longer resides.
I need you to leave, no open rooms in my mind.
Today and every day, I'll let spirit guide.
Certainty emerges, false beliefs subside.

Peace, come and fill me with your gentle escape.
Replace the chaos, fill this void, leave no trace.
Destiny expands within this newfound space.
For with faith, I'll conquer life's challenging phase.

Oh, how sweet the victory and taste,
As I savor, winning this race.

Transparency

Opaque shadows, a cloak of disgrace,
Fragments of glass, subliminal waste.
Guarded and fearful, resisting what awaits,
When confusion is removed clarity remains.

Seek the truth you've long kept at bay.
Unearth the love and laughter gone astray.
Strip away the layers, one by one.
Revealing the principle, a resplendent sun.

Take off your mask, reveal your true form.
No murmurs of falsehood to distort and deform.
In your nakedness, a luminous glow.
Release the troubles and let them all flow.

Opaque shadows, a cloak of disgrace,
Shattered glass, can't dictate.
Guarded and fearful, resisting what awaits,
When confusion is removed clarity remains.

Shifting
Affirmations

I am more efficient each day.

I find ways to be effective in my plans and goal setting.

I am creating organization in every area of my life.

I understand that my environment can influence my mental space therefore, I am willing to take the steps necessary to SHIFT.

I am shifting my mindset to a healthier place.

I am shifting my environment into a healthier space.

I am aligning myself internally and externally.

Everything in my life is shifting for my good.

I will be an active participant in my shift.

The shifting has already begun.

CHAPTER 3
SUNLIGHT & RAINY DAYS

Some things just are…

Growing Pains

Unavoidable.

It must happen.

Unspeakable, our love without a caption.

Irrevocable.

We let it happen, it had to happen.

It tested us.

We didn't run, we faced it.

We faced each other.

Vocalizing.

Internalizing.

Reflecting and recognizing.

Even when there were surprises.

Pain that caused uprisings.

We held on when things were not appetizing.

We learned the imperfections in our perfections.

The weakness in our recollections.

The strength in our forgiveness.

The vividness in our transparency.

The truth of you and me.

The beauty and chaos found within humanity.

We had to go through the growing pains.

On the Outside

From the outside looking in, I stand.

A couple that once flourished, where did it begin?
And where, oh where, will it meet its end?

A weight sleeps heavily upon my chest.
They call it love, but I call it a test.
Together we tried to express love sublime.
Reckless speeds crossed boundaries and time.

Words spoken and battered.
No running faucet to wash away what mattered.
Now splinters of words begin to unroll.
Wait, close your eyes, and regain control.

Grab the change, pay the toll to cross.
This voyage, ain't for the faint, don't get lost.
It's time to communicate, to bridge the divide.
The gate has swung open, inviting strides.

Unfiltered waters now flow before our eyes.
An opportunity to rise above the tides.
No need to react, listen and see.
You were always on the inside, always you and me.

Grief

I hum a melody from deep within.
The depth of mercy has not sunken in.
The tears from my eyes can no longer cry.
The wounded spirit, the lowly sighs.

Unanswered questions linger in the air,
Death offers no reconciliation to those who still care.
Hands raised, seeking a sign,
Yearning for relief in the darkest of nights.

Comfort, when found, is sober and clear,
Happy memories, moments held dear,
Glimmers of laughter, heartbreaks, and strife,
Yearning for solace as I navigate life.

Grasping for a time when this pain eases,
And I can slowly begin to pick up the pieces.
Picking up the fragments, left undone,
And now, I gather them, one by one.

If I Could Rewind Time
Lyrical Reflection

If I could turn back the hands of time,
I'd close my eyes and travel by cosmic design.
To uncover the curse that veiled our sight,
Dividing our spirits into parallel light.

Once dynamic lovers, now strangers, we roam,
Lost in the shadows of what we used to own.
I'd race to that place where our beings aligned,
Where love's flame ignited, unconfined.

In those moments, our faces locked in a gaze,
Our hearts entwined, dancing in love's blaze.
No fear to speak, no holding back our voice,
Building a bond, our connection would rejoice.

I blame myself for losing my independence,
For sacrificing my identity in your presence.
If time could rewind, I'd answer Joy's call,
Laugh freely, be me, and not fear the fall.

No more heaviness, tears flowing without a fight,
Motivated to live, flickering candlelight.
No allowing life's shadow to eclipse who we are,
Listening to other voices, losing sight of our star.

Anger and distance engulfed our cherished space,
Friction and tension created a maze.
I fight for us, feel trapped inside us,
Disconnection, we refuse to hide.

If I could rewind time, I'd kneel and pray,
For a different path and day.
No disarrayed hearts, no strained conversation,
Splitting from this painful separation.

Yet, as I look closer, I realize the truth,
That distance has grown, a deepening groove.
No matter how familiar, we're too far apart,
As we once were, now fragments of the heart.

But I won't retreat into a cocoon of despair,
I'll face the unknown with courage to bear.
Even if time rewound, I wouldn't stay confined,
I'd embark on the present, leaving the past behind.

Dark Shores

In the silence, at the doorway's edge,
Thoughts lingered, waiting to emerge,
Seeking a chance to dive into the unsuspecting,
Where a black hole of thoughts had grown.

It swirled around, and under my bed it dispersed,
A brewing storm of fears, where shadows tread,
Rebels of doubt, plotting their intrusion,
Challenging my plans for self-revolution.

I spoke of truths no one dared to hear,
The darkness that threatened to steal my years,
Questions of burden, existence's plight,
Why am I here, and is it worth the fight?

In solitude, I pondered who would lend an ear,
If I couldn't love myself and my skin hold dear,
Who'd see beyond my pain, my velvet drape,
Love me unconditionally, with boundless grace?

And there were many, I soon discovered,
I was never alone, my fears uncovered,
Kindred souls who'd walked the path before,
Guiding me through dark shores to explore.

I found within me a flicker of light,
A seed yearning to grow, to take flight,
A glimmer of hope to endure the night,
In my heart, I believed things would be alright.

Victim Mentality
Reflection

We have a choice: to stay locked in a victim mentality, convinced that the world is conspiring against us and that only misfortune awaits, or to rise above. We can face cognitive distortions, neglect, trauma, and abuse. We can decide to master the challenges that greet us at our doorsteps. It is essential to realize that we cannot undo the past or turn back time, but we hold the power to choose to let go. Letting go does not imply condoning or excusing what has transpired; it grants us the autonomy to reclaim our power, embracing the present and shaping our future.

In this passage called life, some days may feel endless, and weariness may overcome us. Yet, deep within us is an inherent longing for healing and a better tomorrow. This resilience exposes itself when we open ourselves to new possibilities adding value to each moment. Life itself is a precious gift, as humans we sometimes complicate it. May we find the strength to live on our terms, nurturing the purpose within us since the dawn of time. May our failures become valuable experiences from which we grow, showing ourselves empathy along the way.

Let us acknowledge our strengths, celebrating the unique qualities that make us who we are. Within the unique space we create for ourselves, let healing and growth flourish. May we be empowered to choose our path, elevate above adversity, and manifest the life we envision. As we sojourn, may we consistently hold space for ourselves, allowing wounds to be healed, bodies to rejuvenate, and spirits to soar.

Hold On

I could barely breathe,
Gripping the rubbery wheel,
A grasp on life's breadth.

Cornered from every side,
Imprisoned in this shape,
Metal cages surround,
Reflecting on my internal chase.

Physically and artistically,
Recreating my state,
No escape in sight,
Only speed and a decision to accelerate.

Pressing harder on the gas,
Propelling beyond time and dimension,
A chain reaction,
Impact and darkness, all on my own.

With closed eyes,
 I envisioned the void and nothingness,
A silent existence,
That couldn't bring contentment.

My heart yearned for something simpler, profound,
Peace, elusive like water surging, pouring.

Gravity pulls,
Emotions weigh me down,
Tears stream uncontrollably,
My face, a watery frown.

Streaks of black mascara mingle with my skin,
My lace blouse dissolved, a casualty within.

Amidst this emotional earthquake, I stand isolated,
In the center of an island, unheard and underrated.
Seeking to live, not seeking pity's sway,
In a world quick to judge, opinions are on display.

They idolize hate and cancel humanity's stake,
Love, faith, and hope, where do you abate?
Deferred dreams, making the heart sick and sore,
Is life a treat to savor or just a trick to endure?

Hear me roar amidst the chaos and disaster,
It's my choice to make, I choose to be the master.

Spiraling

I embarrassed myself,
I lost control of my words,
Engulfed by negativity,
Unable to perceive what I heard.

Reacting without accuracy,
Consumed by anger's grip,
My tongue became a weapon,
Every sentence, a sharp trip.

In my misguided dismissal, prejudice took hold,
Creating an enemy where none unfolded.
Turning my back reality left me feeling weak,
Ashamed of my actions, uncertain and meek.

I recognize my wrongs,
The path I chose to tread,
But the words I spewed,
Were filled with hate instead.

Caught in a cycle of dread,
Wondering how I got here,
I understand now,
It was my stubbornness and fear.

Have you ever been there,
Confined by pride's touch?
Abandoning what truly matters,
Fighting too much.

In a moment that called for maturity and grace,
My feelings were valid,
But my actions were misplaced.

It wasn't about stifling who I am at my core,
But rather a call to use my voice for love,
Nothing more.

To construct and uplift,
Rather than manipulate and control,
I seek shelter after the storm I have thrown.

Alone with my thoughts,
No affirmations worth repeating,
A lesson learned,
A moment to love myself in the healing.

Examining the roots,
Of my selfish blindness and rage,
Confronting the hopelessness,
That led me astray on this page.

I reach for my Sage, igniting its glow,
Waving away the smoke, dissipating the fight.
In quiet attestation, I know the right thing to do,
Seeing with purity, uncovering what is true.

Unable to turn back time, I must move ahead,
Learning from this experience,
Growing.

To do better, to be better,
For myself and those I love,
Acknowledging my folly and rising above.

One day at a time...

Perfect Imperfection

As I delve within,
I witness the cracks of life unfold,
Now sealed, love has mended.

The scars that caused deep agony,
Now changed with grace,
Simply a work of art,
Reminders of our strength and percipience.

The thoughts and unease that once held us tight,
Now linger as faint residue, fading out of sight.
They dwell in the distance,
Overshadowed by our will,

To live, to love, to honor our existence.

We are more than what meets the eye,
Divine in this earthly guise,
He sees her beauty; she sees his,
A love that defies.

Perfection found in imperfections,
Embodied as one,
A shared direction, hearts beating with affection,
Never undone.

Auto Pilot
Reflection

Each morning, I would awaken with a sense of purpose and a deep commitment to my role as a wife. For thirteen years, my decisions became driven by the desire to make life easier for those I encountered. Losing myself in exchange.

I avoided conflict at all costs, believing that maintaining peace was my duty for the greater good of humanity. However, the weight of this strained relationship began to take its toll, manifesting as physical, emotional, and mental weights. Despite my attempts to communicate my inner turmoil, my voice faded into the void. In desperation, I started on a campaign of self-discovery, realizing that I was existing in an unhappy situation.

Have you ever found yourself driving in traffic, only to arrive without recollection of the process? Losing awareness of your present state. Becoming detached from our consciousness can become a concern. How many of us have experienced this detachment? It extends beyond overcommitment; it speaks to how we have chosen to move through life. A form of numbing the hurt, turning a blind eye, and disassociating from that situation or relationship.

I recognized my role in this deception and refused to continue to live on autopilot. I was told that my desire for personal happiness and fulfillment was selfish. While others imposed their expectations upon my life without considering my happiness or well-being. Autopilot living had its allure as it required no conscious thought.

After years of dwelling in this state, I questioned how would I function outside of this suffocating conundrum?

It all begins with a bold decision to live. The embracing of the power of presence and intention, consciously shaping our thoughts and actions. We start by showing up for ourselves, honoring our needs, and nurturing our inner child. We start by choosing to live authentically.

In this quest for a life filled with purpose and meaning, let us remember that we are not alone. Together, we unlock the door to a world where every breath is infused with vitality and every step carries the complexity of our true selves. Let's go!

Shadow Work

Unveiling the hidden secrets, long untouched,
Unraveling the unloved parts within our grasp.
Where do we commence this expedition anew?
With gentle steps, introspection ensues.

What molds our thoughts, actions, and inner delight?
Why do we tread the paths where darkness hides?
The inner child whispers, longing to be heard,
In stillness, we listen, her story unfurled.

We survey the problems, unburdening our cross,
Carefully turning pages to make ourselves whole.
Healing takes root; exhaustion finds its relief,
Point blank, finding inner peace.

We feel, we weep, releasing all the pain,
Shame, anger, rejection, once a shield in vain.
Moving forward, creating what lies ahead,
Motivated, weightless, fault-finding shed.

No more excuses, we won't dwell,
Consciously choosing our destiny's lure.
For the power is now contained, it's time to heal,
Clenching our potential, making life surreal.

Now, with prominence and purpose, we fulfill,
Healing the wounds, transmuting with strong will.
Free, we push forth from the past,
Fashioning a moment, forever to last.

I Am Forgiven
Affirmations

I forgive myself for my past mistakes.

I am worthy of forgiveness and peace of mind.

I am forgiven and I forgive myself
unconditionally.

I am deserving of love, compassion, and
understanding.

I forgive myself for any harm I have caused and
strive to make amends where possible.

I am open to receiving forgiveness from others
and extending forgiveness to them.

I am worthy of second chances and
opportunities for redemption.

I am grateful for the healing that forgiveness
brings to my mind, body, and soul.

I am ready to release any resentment or grudges
and live a life filled with forgiveness and harmony.

I embrace the lessons learned from my past and
use them to create a better future.

CHAPTER 4
NURTURED

To care for and encourage growth and development.

The Love I Have

I didn't always love you as I do now,
Doubts once clouded my perception somehow,
Judging your skin, questioning your birth,
Caught in society's standards, not seeing worth.

Hair deemed too curly, laughter too loud,
Society's expectations, I allowed,
But now I see you with eyes renewed,
A glowing soul, strong, and true.

Not defined by others' decree,
I've discovered the real essence of me,
Unapologetically embracing my being,
Uncovering the greatness, I am seeing.

I've found my voice, my joy, my peace,
I'm not lost, I find relief.
In the mirror, I see my true reflection,
A Goddess among men, a majestic connection.

I inhale my magic, exhale with ease,
Rejecting the appeal of the past's striptease.
My life's lessons, my guiding light,
Outshining any Ivy League's might.

I've traveled paths only I could tread,
The sole competition, the self I shed.
For now, I understand the love I possess,
The love for me, I now confess.

All I Need
Reflection

The scent of rain delights my senses, a gentle reminder of the cleansing and nourishment it brings. It draws my mind towards nature, where the Earth diligently cares for all its inhabitants.

The cold seeps through my window, a sense of awakening washes over me while a comforting cup of Zen tea warms my being. In this moment, I find balance where chaos would try to reside.

I release the need for external validation, allowing self-love to cleanse any remnants of past experiences, affirming my inherent value and worth. Surrendering to the present, I stride courageously towards the future, knowing I am never alone.

The boundless love of the Universe surrounds me, and I remain attentive, as the needs required for my flourishing are revealed within the plentifulness of the Earth.

Light of Mine

Shine forth, my little starlight,
Take hold of your radiance,
Please don't hide,
No more hesitance.

Receive the breath of the day,
With confidence and sight,
Proudly carry your tune,
Concealed in the night.

You are not destitute, inside, or out,
You sow seeds of love and reap what you devout,
Know the power you hold,
The love you can bestow.

Unable to ignore the truth inside,
Let your true self show.
Your splendor shines, you set the pace,
Cherish your shine, don't let it fade away,

Do not fret or let your flame of passion consume,
Share your vibrant soul,
With those who respect your bloom.

This light holds immense power,
When embraced,
Illuminate the world,
Leave a lasting trace.

Float On

My voice may not be the loudest in the crowd,

But it carries truth beyond my youth.
Rubies, diamonds, amethyst, and pearls,
Tiger eyes that observe the wisdom of the world.

Been there before no need to rewind,
The teachings etched within the mind.
Aromatics fill the air, a fragrant spell,
Lifting us higher, where our spirits dwell.

Bubble, bubble, bubble up, we rise,
Elevated to new and intense skylines.
Our persons intertwined, in perfect sync,
Defining new beginnings, in matching link.

A sense of self we now regain,
Floating on waves of growth, released from strain.
Bubble, bubble, bubble up, elation soars,
The sunshine's rays warm our cores.

Kindness nourishes and we accept,
For we know what we can control.
Together we flow in unity and grace,
Embracing the power to inhale, up and away.

Authentically Me (prayer-ish)

Cross my T's and dot my I's,
Never leave my heart behind.
Sweet red lips, ice on the wrist,
Sophisticated and complex-ish.

Never settle, show my teeth,
Though inside, I want peace.
Oil my elbows grease my knees,
Pray that God will hear my plea.

Know my secrets, own them well,
Pick them wisely, which ones to tell.
Always friendly, plainly speak,
Always loyal, never cheat.

Look politely, wait my turn,
Ignite the flame and let it burn.
Lovely, Lovely, eyes do tell,
The love I give casts a spell.

Healed and broken, not in two,
There is no handout ever due.
Perfect, perfect, no such thing,
Refuse to pay for watered dreams.

It's dark and pale, night does tell,
I travel to the wishing well.

I say thank you despite the rain,
And pray that mercy will remain.
No face, no mask, I speak my piece,
And pray the sun will rise in the East.

Running slow and walking fast.
I take my mantle and release my past.
I stand firm, unwilling to break.

A new period ascending, what's in view?
In my precision, I walk in my truth.

Authentically.

Recalibrate

Prolific iterations ruminate within my head.
Fighting the congregation, as I lay on the bed.
Memories of glances, lingering stares,
Brief debut on the stage, riveted by dares.

Erasing the writings, correcting the script,
Confronting childhood's shadows, bit by bit.
Until I walked on water, stumbled upon truth,
Unshackled rumors and stepped in the booth.

Talk, talk, listen, and cry.
Releasing all I carried because it was time.
The time has come, the time is here,
Careful where I'm led, oil upon my head.

In silence, surrounded, the clamor shall cease,
Gentle steps forward, walking in peace.
Convictions' intruding, withering, and stale,
Walking away from this repetitive trail.

No vision, no vision, impedes the way,
Detaching from the crowd, finding my sway.

It's time to recalibrate.

Life Choices
Reflection

What makes one person more successful than another person? Do you allow another's success to cause you to be green with envy? Do you celebrate them and let it ignite your passion and motivation towards your goals and desires? We can accomplish certain things independently but there are times when a supportive community is essential to our growth and success.

We should acknowledge the force of inspiration, motivating individuals, and the vast resources that are available. Take a moment to quickly identify these inspiring figures in your life or that you know of and identify the patterns that define them. Often one pattern appears, they make a conscious choice to alter their lives.

We also have the power of choice, shaping our actions and reactions as we go throughout the day. We have the independence to be strategic in our pursuits, avoiding the grip of procrastination that hinders our progress.

In these pivotal moments, we must research the story we have authored about our lives. If you find yourself distant from your aspirations, reflect on the narrative you are telling yourself.

What beliefs and limitations are holding you back? Conversely, if you stand triumphantly in the place you imagined, recall the story that propelled you forward, instilling unwavering determination. The tale you weave within your mind can shape your reality and propel you toward success.

You hold the power of choice, rewrite your story, and let it be the driving force that propels you unwaveringly toward your desired destination.

Choices
Affirmations

I choose to move with clarity and intention throughout my day.

I am empowered to make choices that align with my values and aspirations.

I trust myself to make wise and conscious choices that lead to my growth and happiness.

Each choice I make shapes my reality, and I choose to create a positive and fulfilling life.

I embrace the power of choice and take responsibility for the outcomes in my life.

I make choices that honor my authenticity and bring me closer to my true purpose.

I am confident in my ability to make choices that lead to success and fulfillment.

I trust that every choice I make serves a purpose and contributes to my personal evolution.

I See Her, I Wanna Be Her

Look at her from across the room.
Knowing she is all that.
Confidence is her aroma.
Elegance is her diploma.
Authentic in her glance.
Independent in her stance.

I see her, I wanna be her.

Decisive.
She doesn't aim to please but to lead.
Her vibe is one of the visionaries.
Her battle scars make her complete.

I see her, I wanna be her.

Intuitive.
She understands where she is.
The love she has, the love she gives.
Boundaries set and roads not taken.
Relationships formed and that worth shaking.

I see her, I wanna be her.

Never a stranger, she gathers her strength.
And scopes out the danger.
She hears them as they tell their lies.
They wanna break her, mistake her,
Deny who she is.
She refuses to accept defeat.

I see her, I wanna be her.

Can it be true I see her with my eyes.
She is who she says she is,
I feel it, I know it deep down inside,
Even when others reject the treasure, she provides.

I see her because I am her
I see her because I am her
I see her because I am her...

CHAPTER 5
REDEEMED

To gain or regain possession of...

Societal Layers

It's heavy, loaded, exposed, no holster.
Allocated to a wall like a B2K poster.
Frolicking down the spine like a dragon tattoo.
Bravo, Lifetime, what do we have to do?
Anxious, foresight speaking, cooked sushi on deck.
Forex money leaking, ain't quite there, not yet.
Protest, disruption, and equator revelations.
Tupac, turmoil, denial, where do we stand?
Not wanting to occupy any other places.
Nations erupting immediately,
Watch who the enemy embraces.
Identity, humility, prejudice, and hate.
Rocks are ready to be thrown, as you enter the gate.
Predicated ignorance.
Programmed lies.
Sexuality summed up to below one's thighs.
Dating apps, Cash apps, and liquid transactions.
Societal dysfunction.
Who chooses this madness?
Will we cater to affliction or denial of living?
Will we right our wrongs first?
Ourselves, have we forgiven?

Conflicted Affection
Lyrical Reflection

I admire you, seeing celestial wonders within,
But you find strategies to belittle, call it a sin.
You misplace my value, diminishing my worth,
To uplift yourself, casting shadows on my birth.

You claim to love, yet your actions contradict,
Leaving me confused and feeling conflicted.
You say you want me by your side, in your life,
But you undermine and hide me, causing strife.

Instead of nurturing my spirit, you seek to destroy,
Competing instead of communicating is a ploy.
Tears dry, healing compromised, distance grows,
Denying love and surprises, it clearly shows.

I see the gold that resides within you, evermore
To love me is not a weakness, it makes us whole.
I unbind the cords of deprivation,
My love for you stays unstripped with devotion.

Disregarded and abandoned, I still hold you dear,
Even when reprimanded, our bond is sincere.
But I see disdain for my skin in your eyes,
The same skin that brought you forth, no disguise.

I carried, nurtured you, and made sacrifices too,
Yet you only glimpse my beauty in a limited view.
Judgments and possessions, reduced to the core,
I pray, respect, and offer mercy and more.

I see beyond your scars, hidden tears, and strife,
Beyond the systemic plan, seeking unity in life.
In the face of injustice, our love stands high,
Day or night, we rise, breaking down every wall.

They say I don't need my man or brother, that's a lie,
For you, I'll always fight, our union won't die.
Together, we transcend transgenerational pain,
In solidarity, our love prevails, no need to explain.

Not Enough
Reflection

It's fascinating how, in the face of relationship challenges, we often succumb to the belief that we are inadequate. When, we are not just good enough but truly exceptional.

We possess an abundance of qualities, talents, and love to offer.

However, it's essential to recognize that the other person may lack the capacity to fully appreciate, receive, or reciprocate all that we bring to the table.

Every experience, whether filled with joy or heartache, is an opportunity for growth. We give and reciprocate, learning valuable lessons. Coming to understand that some relationships are destined to be transient.

Through it all, we must affirm within ourselves that we are enough. We are complete and whole, deserving of love, respect, and contentment.

So, let go of self-doubt and recognize your inherent worth. You are more than enough, and the right relationships, those that support your authentic self, will come into your life at the perfect time.

Trust in your enoughness and allow yourself to thrive!

Intimate Relationships
Affirmations

I am worthy of having intimate, trusting relationships with others.

I decide who I share my intimate space with for it is safe and mutually reciprocated.

I attract and nurture relationships built on trust, respect, and emotional intimacy.

I communicate openly and honestly, fostering trust and deepening the intimacy in my relationships.

I am worthy of experiencing profound love, trust, and intimacy in my partnerships.

I release any fears or barriers that hinder the growth of trust and intimacy in my relationships.

I create a safe and secure space for vulnerability and intimacy to thrive in my connections.

I choose partners who value and prioritize trust and intimacy, cultivating fulfilling relationships.

I am grateful for the deep level of trust and intimacy that exists in my relationships.

Arise

She discovered herself,
Between life's sprawling pages.
Each chapter outspread,
Revealing diverse intersections.

What does she dare to dream?
Which direction beckons her?
In newly found freedom,
She becomes whole, even for a fleeting moment.

She leaps freely, overwhelmed in emotions,
Flowing as the sea.
Grateful for her rightful place,
She listens intently to her inner voice.

Looking beyond traditions,
That once hampered her destiny.
Thinking others knew what was best,
Only to wake to rejection.

Wrapped like a mummy, not anymore
Words spoken harshly still sting,
Unwanted touches are fading memories.
She recognizes that she is one of a kind.

The optimism she longs to materialize,
No longer distant facets of the past.
She stands, refusing to be designed,
By what's left behind, she redefines.

Using her past as fuel,
To realign her position in the universe.
She rehearses who she truly is,
Affirming her new beginning is not a facade.

It belongs to her to welcome, own,
Her faith empowers and uplifts her.
Nightly meditations bring visions and reconciliation,
Her walls witness her triumphs and humble defeats.

Valiant and beautiful in her sight,
This is not a sad story but a divine restoration.
A fight to overcome complacency and sorrow,
Fast forward past the old songs, seizing what she can.

ARISE, for pity, has no place here,
Her strength is deeply ingrained.
No two stories are alike,
She observes, taking the necessary steps.

For a brand-new day, she insists,
Unstoppable, approaching the challenge.
Can you feel the energy in the air?
Can you recognize her renewed mindset?

Can you see her reflection in yourself?
Then ARISE...

I Rise
Affirmations

I rise today with intention, purpose, influence,
health, wealth, and love.

I rise above any challenges that come my way.

I rise above self-doubt and embrace my worthiness.

I rise with courage and determination in the face of
adversity.

I rise to create the life I desire, filled with joy, love,
and abundance.

I speak life even in the moments when things look
barren because I know that seeds take time to grow, to
produce.

I arrive on this day present, grounded, and alert with
expectation and favor!

Nature's Rebirth

The Earth's call resonates deep within my being.
Whispered by the wind, sharing its many seasons.
Fire warms and ignites ashes of the past, insights,
Water flows and cleanses.

Blood-stained streets tell stories of survival.
Laughter veiling tears, a delicate balance.
Inward and outward, destined for a cause.
Healing beckons, yet no time for a pause.

The path I tread is essential and clear.
Thoughts evolving, existential and sincere.
Resisting negativity, ensuing progress,
No gatekeeper, but a force of togetherness.

Nature patiently waits, eager for my stay.
To learn its wisdom, reflect on grace.
Together we unite, divinely combined.
Order emerges, it's time to find.

The now of my purpose, the truth of my being.
Uncovering time, the path worth seeing.
With nature's guidance and my spirit allied,
I step forward, ready to fulfill what's mine.

Together-Together-Together
Divine-Divine-Divine
Order-Now
Find Me

Birthing Creation

Breasts dangling, gently swaying,
Nurturing life, a nation's creation.
No room for complaints or dismay,
Midwives gather, guiding.

Panting, screams, breaths shallow and deep.
Bearing down a price so steep.
Tears, blood, and sweat confine,
Amid beauty, courage finds.

Pushing forward, reclaiming the womb,
Songs of chanting, dispelling the gloom.
No longer enslaved, wade into the light,
A powerful passage, reclaiming our rights.

Reputation

Amid the night's encase,
Where shadows mingle with grace,
In darkness, the earth yields,
And the womb produces life.

Misunderstood, its reputation,
Feared by words of false inflation,
Yet in its depths, a revelation,
Life emerges with elation.

A womb of possibilities untold,
Where miracles and love bellow,
A transient state, a threshold,
Where inspiration takes hold.

Darkness, void of expectations,
Liberates from societal imitations,
Reflecting on an inner revolution,
Finding solace in its contemplations.

A realm of dualities entangled,
Where beauty's heart is defined,
Boundless, unrestricted,
In the darkness, self-restoration we find.

No labels, no fabricated tales,
Embracing spirit, as darkness pales,
Returning to self, where peace prevails,
A roaming where authenticity sails.

For darkness, despite its reputation,
Holds secrets of profound creation,
In its arms, a sacred invitation,
To rediscover our fascination.

Redeemed

Sitting in solace, I recaptured my peace.
Formulated plans, calculated dreams.
Room for my vision, remove black and white.
Technicolor movements, I choose to live my life.

I'm not running away from my truth.
I must live it, no, not you.
I must love it; this is my choice to make.
I must accept it if it's something I can't change.

I lift my head, refuse to be ashamed.
The captivating audience, no need to blame.
Lingering loyally, firm in my stance.
I acknowledge life's lessons I choose to dance.

Celebrating me, a glorious day beckons.
Mercies sent down and grace abounds too.
Receiving streams and manifesting dreams.
Grateful, blessed, knowing I'm redeemed.

I Am the Ocean

Beneath the ocean's depths, the earth lies unrested,
Tainted by the struggles of ancestors,
Oppressed, and tested.
Forced on a voyage, a journey not of their choice,
Their stories carried on waves, a haunting voice.

Anguished cries echo through the winds of time,
Aching for distant lands, a longing to find.
The tormenting decisions of the past,
Impact lives, shaping a world so vast.

Reaching the shore, no peace is found,
The weight of history is heavy and profound.
Unable to fathom what it means for me,
Gazing into the ocean, deep.

Breathing life into dreams once conceived,
With the tenacity of those who believed.
Progressive and determined, with prophetic cries,
Providing solace, standing strong by their side.

Their presence is felt, a testament of grace,
Once hidden from blind eyes,
Now revealed in this watery space.
But where does mercy lead on this sacred shore?
Where dignity, lost and found, seeking to restore.

Their struggles echo through the distance of time,
Their spirit resides in every crest and rhyme.
With reverence, I honor their enduring fight,
Their sacrifice fuels my resolve.

I am the ocean, it courses within my soul,
A part of me, where ancestral stories unfold.
In that sacred place, my forebears paid the cost,
To break the shackles, to reclaim what was lost.

CHAPTER 6
GROUNDED

Finding Stability…

Today, I Choose
Affirmations

Today, I choose to master my thoughts.

Today, I choose to master my time.

Today, I choose to master my day!

Perception

I presented you with roses in full bloom,
Yet all you saw were the thorns.
Diamonds I offered, treasures worn and true,
Yet you criticized, dismissing their value.

I saw your inner beauty, a rare sight to behold,
But you accused me of being fake and cold.
I recognized your struggles, I saw you weep,
Yet you sought to break me, my spirit to keep.

In my quest for love and blessings to impart,
It somehow turned into a mess, a fractured heart.
But now I digress, accepting what can't be changed,
Knowing our eyes won't meet, pathways estranged.

Your eyes will never meet mine, unable to see,
Your mind clouded by transgressions,
Your heart whispers only what it holds dear,
Lost in toxic realms, refusing to be clear.

I call upon the winds from every direction,
Boundaries are set for mind and heart protection.
I know my truth, I trust in who I am,
Offering you energy and peace was no sham.

I offered you my love,
An olive branch from my tree.
Experiences abound through the waves of growth,
Call me victory.

Sunlight refracts,
In hope I will remain,
Even after this subtraction,
I will still be okay.

Collapse

In the stillness, perched on the edge,
I navigate the trials, my survival pledge.
Words like sledgehammers shape my fate,
Manifesting strength, I refuse to abdicate.

Mind and will be liberated, sanctions no more,
Breathing easily on wings, I soar.
In this crash course of self-navigation,
I find my footing, embracing emancipation.

Complex relations, hidden minefields untamed,
I rise above the fire, unscathed and unblamed.
No empire's collapse can hinder my desire,
As I seek truth, undeterred by deceptive attire.

Attention seekers surround themselves with lies,
But I march to my beat, where wisdom arrives.
Conspiracies crumble, their effects grow numb,
I leave the games behind, a positive outcome.

So, find another foe, if you must engage,
For I refuse to stay down on this life's stage.

Uncovered

Discover me during my growth,
Boldly walking with my antidote.
With rugged boots and a fancy tote,
I wander the streets where dreams and reality float.

Here, epiphany speaks softly, its sage advice,
Teaching me to avoid Deja Vu's surprise.
No messing with me I'm focused and driven,
A mission birthed, on a plane higher than heaven.

My abilities, thoughts, and moves coincide,
For I will manifest what was assigned.
Witness a greatness, a unique one's endeavor,
A spirit no longer bound, celestial tether.

Interstellar energies and frequencies high,
Vibrations rising, traversing the sky.
Don't avert your gaze, listen to my plea,
This transcends us, it's to a greater degree.

Beyond you and me, it writes future tales,
For generations to come, as time prevails.
Are we willing to dismantle what's old,
Set ablaze the foundations of hate and hypocrisy?

Let us stop jumping like puppets on strings,
Denial demands reprisal, truth clearly rings.
No more catering to a broken system's needs,
Band-aids won't cure societal misdeeds.

We are the currency, gaining traction with ease.
We are the catalysts of evolution, aboundingly.
Empowered by unity, we shape a new decree.
Organized by purpose, our impact spans the seas.

Let us speak, unafraid of what is ahead,
Fear has no place when we're united instead.
It is they who fear our collective might,
Together, we define what's true and right.

So, who are we, you may ask?
We are the embodiment of a courageous task.
We are the voice, the strength, the driving force,
United,
We shape a future,
Where love takes its course.

Process
Affirmations

There is a download that is taking place in my life.

I understand my present state, yet I keep my eyes

on my end goal(s)

knowing that what I face in between is the process.

The process is only meant to strengthen me, teach

me, build me, and prepare me for what is already

mine.

I trust the process of growth and renovation in

my life.

I am open to learning and evolving through the

process.

I celebrate small victories and milestones in my

process.

I release control and surrender to the wisdom of

the process.

I honor and respect the process, knowing that it

has valuable lessons for me.

I accept the process.

I embrace the process.

In the Garden

In the depths of introspection, I found love.
Not defined by others, I rose above,
Expectations and demands, I set myself free.
Reclaiming my life, enchanting identity.

Once overshadowed by the dreams of others,
I lost sight of myself, my true colors,
But now I blossom, a radiant floret,
Taking root.

No more sacrificing, no more enabling,
I refuse to be a victim of love's mishandling,
Like a trampled flower, I emerge from the ground,
Under the moonlight, a new strength I found.

Patiently waiting for the sun's healing rays,
It arrived unexpectedly, my gospel's saving grace.
Dusting off my petals, quenching my thirst,
The sun's love was pure, it came to me first.

A kaleidoscope of love, nurturing my blues,
Striking and magical, mystical tunes.
In my darkness, I discovered growing faith.
A rebirth, guiding me to a bountiful space.

Now I walk a captivating path in the garden of life.
Rooted in self-love, liberated from strife.
Not persuaded by those who seek to use.
I protect my garden and its mesmerizing hues.

Entangled

It's a slow burn,
As you pull the leather against my skin.
I can't speak,
The pain and passion keep me in conflict.

I'm enraptured by the thought of your hands,
Discovering my continent.
Your passion, supersedes shades of gray,
Mutual consent for this role play.

Temperatures quickly elevate, here we lay,
Like a display.
Your anatomy intercepts mine,
Creating chemistry.

$P=MV$, there's no gravity,
Momentum accumulates as we lose sanity.
Lost in a vortex, forget vanity,
Savagely, forcefully engaged, and entangled.

Sexuality
Affirmations

I cultivate sexual wellness in my life.

I live, love, and engage in sexual behaviors according to my values.

I deserve love and respect in all aspects of my sexual life.

I trust my instincts and communicate my desires and boundaries confidently.

I release any shame, judgment, or guilt associated with my sexuality and embrace self-acceptance.

I engage in open and honest conversations about sexual health, boundaries, and consent.

I nurture a healthy and positive relationship with my body and sexuality.

I release any past traumas or negative experiences that may hinder my sexual well-being.

Self-Exploration

In the ebb and flow, I move on.
Questioning why and how I've grown.
A silent promise I made to try,
To find balance, regulate my inner eye.

What caused this imbalance I ponder,
Fear of promises and no happily-ever-after,
Years marked by moments of despair,
Tears unprocessed, scars I wear.

The frustrations and wounds that test my will,
Triggering anger, a softness that spills.
How do I stop this leaky pipe's flow?
Progress and regress, a dance I know.

Linked like railroad tracks, a constant motion,
With determination, I'll create a new notion.
Like an earthquake, I seek transformation,
To be loosed from pessimism's creation.

No blame to cast, faceless complaints,
Realizing it's just me and my restraints.
I won't despise the process of rising,
Moving forward, myself arriving.

Though painful to be born again,
I face the challenge, my strength I'll defend.
I decide how my days will be,
As I voyage inward, finding the real me.

Walk With Me

Come, take a stroll by my side,
Our fingers interlocked,
As we wander along the shore,
Where sandy paths oblige.

Marvel at the azure waters,
Feel the gentle breezes touch,
Caressing our sun-kissed skin,
It reminds us of love's clutch.

Look into my eyes,
As I peer into your window,
In this peaceful trance,
Our hearts become the scroll.

Transfixed and tangled,
Lost in a ball of affection,
I taste the sweetness of your lips,
A passionate expression.

Together, we discover simplicity,
Anchored by love's grace,
Shielded from negativity,
Place your hands upon my waist.

Communication as our stronghold,
We defy all adverse tides,
Immunized against the world,
As love becomes our prize.

Sista Friend

Sistas in sync, our thoughts entwined,
Halls resound with laughter, joy undefined.
Tears happily flow, our emotions spill,
Unfazed by onlookers, our connection is real.

Club hopping, hand clapping, a shopping spree,
We pray, we cry, finding inner peace.
Meditating, rising above, lifted by grace,
A sista friend for each life phase.

She's my number one fan, a cheerleader true,
Supporting till the end, whatever we go through.
Whether it's a loan or a bobby pin's need,
My sista friend is there, a loyal creed.

Let's venture on shopping trips side by side,
With lace fronts rearranged, we stride.
Loyalty personified, a treasure so rare,
She speaks truth, a shade thrower with care.

In storms of life, my trusted umbrella,
A fighter, ready, no matter the battle.
I hold deep love for my sista friend goals,
A bond eternal, that's how we roll.

Through ups and downs, we persist and mend,
Forgiving, growing, as our rhythms blend.
With her by my side, I stay on my feet,
Her wisdom and advice, in heartache, complete.

Her arms are open, ready to lend a hand,
As I reciprocate, a symbiotic band.
Together, we redefine the rules of the game,
She's a gift for which I'm grateful every day!

I Am Here
Affirmations

I am here, grounded and connected to my body.

I understand that I was created with purpose,

passion, determination, and resilience.

I am present in this moment, fully aware of my

surroundings.

I am here, embracing the opportunities and

challenges that come my way.

I am here, ready to learn, grow, and evolve.

I am here, radiating my authentic self to the

world.

I am here, grateful for the experiences that

have shaped me.

I am not here to perform but to fulfill.

I Am Here.

Destiny

You were never a mistake, born with intent,
Scars are emblems of resilience, they represent.
Your presence is crucial, shaping life's course,
Take the seeds given, nurture your own force.

Abundance shall bless some, while others parade,
Whatever you plant will not be in vain.
Some fruit will be for you and some to share,
Nurture your garden with love and care.

Not all may possess what's sown in the earth,
Man's design wasn't meant for omniscient birth.
With glimpses of what lies ahead, intuition leads,
Embrace patience for now, open minds proceed.

Sharing with you is a profound privilege, I say,
May you extend it to others along the way.
Destiny calls, have you heard this before,
Are you still waiting on the other side of the door?

Are you asking for more but refusing to listen?
Do you know the way, but you remain hidden?
Destiny beckons, time won't stand still,
Unveil the door, before it fades, against your will.

This world can be cruel but don't be afraid,
Create, for it is your gift, your love, and praise.
Craft with purpose, fueled by passion's flame,
Even if one soul is touched, a life will be changed.

TO BE CONTINUED...

RESOURCES

Seeds...

The National Domestic Violence Hotline:

1-800-799-7233 (SAFE) www.ndvh.org

National Dating Abuse Helpline:

1-866-331-9474 www.loveisrespect.org

Crisis Text Line:

Text HOME to 741741 from anywhere in the USA.

Crisis Text Line is here for any crisis.

National Sexual Assault Hotline:

1-800-656-4673 www.rainn.org

National Suicide & Crisis Line:

988 (CALL or TEXT)

National Human Trafficking Resource Center:

Call: 1-888-373-7888

Text: HELP to BeFree (233733)

https://humantraffickinghotline.org/en/get-help

National Center for Victims of Crime:

www.victimsofcrime.org

National Coalition for the Homeless:

www.nationalhomeless.org

LGBTQ+ National Hotline:

Call: 1-888-843-4567

The Network/La Red Abuse Hotline for LGBTQ+,

Kink, and Polyamorous folks:

24/7 Call: 1-800-832-1901

Visit: www.tnlr.org

Trans Lifeline:

Call: 877-565-8860

Visit: www.translifeline.org

Women's Law: www.womenslaw.org

ABOUT THE AUTHOR

Maritta Colbert, affectionately known as MK, is a Jamaican American creative entrepreneur who wears many hats with grace and determination. As a social worker, life coach, author, poet, film producer, and fierce advocate for prison reform, mental health, and LGBTQ+ allyship, she brings her down-to-earth demeanor to every endeavor.

MK believes in practical solutions that create tangible changes in individuals' lives and relationships. She understands the transformative power of love, the significance of healing, and the value of embracing one's true self. With a background and education in business management and a master's degree in social work, MK has pursued her academic passions alongside her creative pursuits. Her love for helping others, film production, performing arts, and the mystical arts has led her to achieve certifications as a Therapeutic Art Life Coach, Reentry Specialist, and Numerology Practitioner. As a co-producer, MK has made significant contributions to two short films, "LiME" and "Dooley Does Murder," in collaboration with Project429 under the name Maritta Kachele. Moreover, she is a visionary and the founder of High Profession Society, a groundbreaking social welfare non-profit organization slated to launch in the summer of 2025. MK's personal journey has been marked by her experiences with trauma, but she has triumphed over adversity and strives each day to become the best version of herself. Embracing her perfect imperfections, she remains humble and open, eager to learn from others and the lessons life presents. Throughout her self-exploration, her commitment to serving others remains resolute, illuminating her path with unwavering dedication.

For bookings, workshops, coaching sessions, and speaking
engagements visit me at
www.icreatemy.life

Like, follow, and share at:
IG: @MarittaKachele

Thank you for your continued support of the arts.